THE ZULU ARMY

AND

ZULU HEA

C000052441

———❧———

COMPILED FROM INFORMATION OBTAINED FROM THE
MOST RELIABLE SOURCES,

AND PUBLISHED,

BY DIRECTION OF THE LIEUT.-GENERAL
COMMANDING,

FOR THE

INFORMATION OF THOSE UNDER HIS COMMAND.

———◆———

SECOND EDITION, REVIZED.

———◆———

The Naval & Military Press Ltd

in association with

The National Army Museum, London

Published jointly by

The Naval & Military Press Ltd

Unit 10 Ridgewood Industrial Park,
Uckfield, East Sussex,
TN22 5QE England

Tel: +44 (0) 1825 749494
Fax: +44 (0) 1825 765701

www.naval-military-press.com
www.military-genealogy.com
www.militarymaproom.com

and

The National Army Museum, London

www.national-army-museum.ac.uk

Printed and bound in Great Britain by
CPI Antony Rowe, Chippenham and Eastbourne

*In reprinting in facsimile from the original, any imperfections are inevitably reproduced
and the quality may fall short of modern type and cartographic standards.*

THE ZULU ARMY.

The Zulu army, which may be estimated at from 40,000 to 50,000 men, is composed of the entire nation capable of bearing arms.

Formation of the Zulu army.

The method employed in recruiting its ranks is as follows:— At short intervals, varying from two to five years, all the young men who have during that time attained the age of fourteen or fifteen years, are formed into a regiment, which, after a year's probation, during which they are supposed to pass from boyhood and its duties to manhood, is placed at a military kraal or head-quarters. In some cases they are sent to an already existing kraal, which is the head-quarters of a corps or regiment, of which they then become part; in others, especially when the young regiment is numerous, they build a new military kraal. As the regiment grows old, it generally has one or more regiments embodied with it, so that the young men may have the benefit of their elders' experience, and, when the latter gradually die out, may take their place and keep up the name and prestige of their military kraal. In this manner corps are formed, often many thousands strong, such, for instance, as the Undi.

Under this system, then, the Zulu army has gradually increased, until at present it consists of twelve corps, and two regiments, each possessing its own military kraal. The corps necessarily contain men of all ages, some being married and wearing the head ring, others unmarried; some being old men scarcely able to walk, while others are hardly out of their teens. Indeed, five of these corps are now composed of a single regiment each, which has absorbed the original but practically non-existent regiment to which it had been affiliated.

Its present divisions.

Each of these fourteen corps or regiments have the same internal formation. They are in the first place divided equally into two wings—the right and the left—and in the second

Internal formation.

are sub-divided into companies from ten to two hundred in number, according to the numerical strength of the corps or regiment to which they belong, and which is estimated in the accompanying table at sixty men each, with the exception of the Nkobamakosi regiment, which averages seventy men to the company.

How officered. Each corps or regiment, possessing its own military kraal, has the following officers: one commanding officer (called the induna yesibaya 'sikulu), one second in command (called the induna yohlangoti), who directly commands the left wing, and two wing officers (called the induna yesicamelo yesibaya 'sikulu, and the induna yesicamelo yohlangoti). Besides the above there are company officers, consisting of a captain, and from one to three junior officers, all of whom are of the same age as the men they command, while in the case of a corps the C.O. of each regiment composing it takes rank next to its four great officers when he is himself not of them.

Uniform. The usual regimental dress and distinguishing marks will be found in the accompanying table, but it is to be noted that during the present war no ornaments or distinguishing marks of any kind, save the difference in shields, have been made use of by the Zulus. The chief distinction is between married and unmarried men. No one in Zululand, male or female, is permitted to marry without the direct permission of the King, and when he allows a regiment to do so, which is not before the men are about forty years of age, they have to shave the crown of the head, and to put a ring round it, and then they become one of the "white" regiments, carrying white shields, &c., in contradistinction to the "black" or unmarried regiments, who wear their hair naturally, and have coloured shields.

Statistics of the Zulu army. The total number of regiments in the Zulu army is thirty-three, of whom eighteen are formed of men with rings on their heads, and fifteen of unmarried men. Seven of the former are composed of men over sixty years of age, and their numbers are not given in the accompanying list, so that for practical purposes there are not more than twenty-six Zulu regiments able to take the field, numbering altogether 40,400. Of these 22,500 are between twenty and thirty years of age, 10,000 between thirty and forty, 3,400 between forty and fifty, and 4,500 between fifty and sixty years of age. From which it will be seen the mortality in Zululand is unusually rapid.

Drill. Drill—in the ordinary acceptation of the term—is unknown among the Zulus; the few simple movements which they perform with any method, such as forming a circle of companies or regiments, breaking into companies or regiments from the circle, forming a line of march in order of companies, or in close order of regiments, not being deserving of the name. Their skirmishing is, however, extremely good, and is performed even under a heavy fire with the utmost order and regularity. The officers have also their regulated duties and responsibilities, according to their rank, and the men lend a ready obedience to their orders.

As might be expected, a savage army like that of Zululand neither has nor requires much commissariat or transport. The former consists of three or four days' provisions, in the shape of maize or millet, and a herd of cattle, proportioned to the distance to be traversed, accompanies each regiment. The latter consists of a number of lads who follow each regiment, carrying the sleeping mats, blankets, and provisions, and assisting to drive the cattle. *Commissariat and Transport.*

When a Zulu army on the line of march comes to a river in flood, and the breadth of the stream which is out of their depth does not exceed from ten to fifteen yards, they plunge in in a dense mass, holding on to one another, those behind forcing them forward, and thus succeed in crossing with the loss of a few of their number. *Mode of crossing rivers.*

In the event of hostilities arising between the Zulu nation and any other (unless some very sudden attack was made on their country), messengers would be sent, travelling night and day if necessary, by the King, to order the men to assemble in regiments at their respective military kraals, where they would find the commanding officer ready to receive them. *How regiments are assembled at their head-quarters.*

When a corps or regiment has thus congregated at its head-quarters, it would, on receiving the order, proceed to the King's kraal. Before marching, a circle or *umkumbi* is formed inside the kraal, each company together, their officers in an inner ring—the first and second in command in the centre. The regiment then proceeds to break into companies, beginning from the left hand side, each company forming a circle, and marching off, followed by boys carrying provisions, mats, &c. The company officers march immediately in rear of their men, the second in command in rear of the left wing, and the C.O. in rear of the right. *Order of march.*

On arriving at the King's kraal each regiment encamps on its own ground, as no two regiments can be trusted not to fight if encamped together. The following ceremonies are then performed in his presence :—All the regiments being formed into an immense circle or *umkumbi*, a little distance *Ceremonies previous to war.*

from the King's kraal, the officers forming an inner ring surrounding the chief officers and the King, together with the doctors and medicine basket. A doctored beast is then killed, it is cut into strips, powdered with medicine, and taken round to the men by the chief medicine man, the soldiers not touching it with their hands, but biting a piece off the strip held out to them. They are then dismissed for the day, with orders to assemble in the morning. The next day early they all take emetics, form an *umkumbi*, and are again dismissed. On the third day they again form an *umkumbi* of regiments, are then sprinkled with medicine by the doctors, and receive their orders through the chief officer of state present, perhaps receiving an address from the King, after which they start on their expedition.

Order of march on an expedition. Previous to marching off, the regiments re-form companies under their respective officers, and the regiment selected by the King to take the lead advances. The march is in order of companies for the first day, after which it is continued in the *umsila* (or path), which may be explained by likening it to one of our divisions advancing in line of brigade columns, each brigade in mass; each regiment in close column; the line of provision bearers, &c., move on the flank; the intervals between heads of columns vary according to circumstances, from several miles to within sight of each other; constant communication is kept up by runners. The march would be continued in this order, with the exception that the baggage and provision bearers fall in rear of the column on the second day; and that the cattle composing the commissariat are driven between them and the rearmost regiment, until near the enemy. The order of companies is then resumed, and, on coming in sight, the whole army again forms an *umkumbi*, for the purpose of enabling the Commander-in-Chief to address the men, and give his final instructions, which concluded, the different regiments intended to commence the attack do so as shown in the plate attached.

Reserve. A large body of troops, as a reserve, remain seated with their backs to the enemy; the commanders and staff retire to some eminence with one or two of the older regiments (as extra reserves). All orders are delivered by runners.

Experience during the present war has shown that, although the above customs were old and the Zulu nation had not been at war for many years, yet there has been little or no change made in them, except in the matter of ornaments, the use of which has been almost entirely discarded. Their method of marching, attack formation, &c., remain the same as before the introduction of fire-arms among them.

THE ZULU ARMY
IN
ATTACK FORMATION.

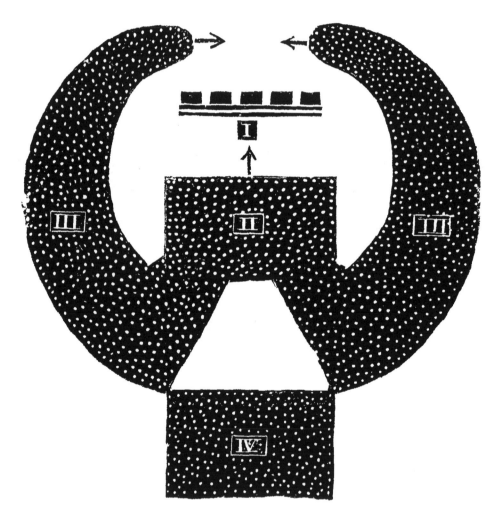

I. The supposed Enemy.

II. The *Chest* of the Army.

III. The *Horns* of the Army.

IV. The Reserve, or *Loins* of the Army.

Corps, or Regiment having a Military Kraal.	Regiment composing Corps.	English Meaning of Name.	Who Raised by.	Name of Commanding Officer.	Name and Position of Military Kraal forming Head Quarters of Corps or Regiment.
*Usixepi			Tyaka	Nqokwane	Usixepi, abont six miles N.N.E. of the Emtonjaneni.
	Nokenke	The " Dividers "	Umpande	Umzilikazi	Usixepi
*Mbelebele		The "Litigious"	Tyaka		Mbelebeleni, on the E. bank of the Black Umfolosi, about 20 miles N.N.E. of the Ondine.
	Umhlanga	The " Reeds "	Umpande		Mbelebeleni
*Umlambo-ngwenya		" Alligator Swamp "	Tyaka	Umfusi	Umlambongwenya, close to the Ondine
	Umxapo	The " Sprinklers "	Umpande		Umlambongwenya
*Udukuza		The " Wanderers "	Tyaka	Makide	Udukuza, between the Mtonjaneni and the Usixepi
	Iqwa	" Frost "	Umpande		Udukuza

Age of Men.	Number of Men in Regiment.	Number of Men in Corps.	Distinguishing Regimental Marks.	Remarks.
80			Band of otter skin round forehead; blue crane feather in centre of forehead; ear-flaps of green monkey skin; shields, white, with large black spots.	All the old regiments wear much the same war dress. The principal men wear a short kilt of civet and green monkey skin tied round the waist, and descending half way to the knee. All the old regiments of Tyaka and most of those of Dingane, are mere skeletons; their names, however, being retained, and their numbers augmented by fresh levies. Thus the Usixepi consists of the Nokenke regiment, the original levy having all but died out.
		2000		
30	2000		Band of leopard skin round forehead (sometimes of otter); two plumes of the Kafir finch on head, pointing backward; ear-flaps of green monkey skin; bunches of white cow-tails hanging from neck down chest and back; shields, black (many have shields of black and white).	The Nokenke were at the action at Sandhlwana on January 22, 1879, forming the Zulu right centre, and at Kambula Hill, March 29, 1879.
78			Dress same as Usixepi; shields, white with red spots.	
		1000		
28	1000		Band of leopard skin round forehead; bunches of black ostrich feathers on front of head, surmounted by several white ostrich feathers; ear-flaps of green monkey skin; bunches of white cow-tails suspended from the neck, and hanging down chest and back; shields, black, with a white spot below.	The Umhlanga were at the action at Sandhlwana on January 22, 1879, being with the Umcityu Regt., 1,400 strong.
75			Dress and shields same as the Usixepi.	
35	2000	2000	Band of leopard skin round forehead (some have otter); plumes of black and white ostrich feathers on head; a bunch of split Kafir finch (sakabuli) feathers at the back of head; ear-flaps of green monkey skin, and bunches of white cow-tails hanging from neck over chest and back; shields, black (some are red, some are spotted).	The Umxapo were at the action at the Nyezane on January 22, 1879.
73			Dress and shields the same as the Usixepi.	
		500		
35	500		Band of leopard skin on forehead; large bunch of split black ostrich feathers on the head, surmounted by plumes of long white ostrich feathers; ear-flaps of green monkey skin; bunches of white cow-tails suspended round neck and hanging down chest and back; shields, black (some are red and white).	The Iqwa were with the Umxapo at Nyezane, January 22, 1879.

Corps, or Regiment having a Military Kraal.	Regiments composing Corps.	English Meaning of Name.	Who Raised by.	Name of Commanding Officer.	Name and position of Military Kraal forming Head Quarters of Corps or Regiments.
*Bulawayo		Place of Killing.	Tyaka	Ngengasilwane	Kwa Bulawayo, about four miles W.N.W. of the Ondine
	Nsugamgeni	Name of a hill in Zululand, above the junction of the Blcod and Buffalo Rivers.	Umpande 5	Umunye	Kwa Bulawayo
*Udhlambedhlu		"Ill-tempered"	Dingane	Ugodide	Udhlambedhlweni about six miles E. of the Usixepi
	*Ngwekwe	A crooked stick	Umpande 6		Udhlambedhlweni
	*Ngulubi or Mhlenivu	The "Pigs"	Umpande 7		Udhlambedhlweni
Nodwengu	Mkulutyane	Straight lines.	Dingane	Mundula	Nodwengu, close to Ondine
	* Umsikaba	Name of river in North of Swaziland	Umpande 8		Nodwengu
	Udududu		Umpande 9		Nodwengu
	Mbubi	Lion	Umpande 10	Utyani	Nodwengu
	* Isanqu	Vaal River	Umpande 11		Isanqweni, close to Undine
* Udabaka-ombi		The affair of Ombi	Dingane	Mawhanqa	Undabakombi, on the spur S. of the Ishlalo hill, about eight miles N.E. of the Ondine.
	* Umkusi	Name of a river in Zululand	Dingane		Undabakaombi

Age of Men.	Number of Men in Regiment.	Number of Men in Corps.	Distinguishing Regimental Marks.	Remarks.
70		1000	Dress same as the Usixepi ; shields, white, and white and red.	Kwa Bulawayo was the principal place of execution used by Tyaka.
25	1000		Dress same as Iqwa : shields, black, with white spot on lower side.	The Nsugamgeni were with the Umxapo at Nyezane, January 22, 1879.
68		1500	Band of otter skin round forehead ; two blue crane feathers (sometimes one only) on either side of the head ; ear-flaps of green monkey skin ; bunches of white cow-tails hanging from neck and covering chest and back ; shields, white, with black or red spots.	The Udhlambedhlu were Dingane's chief regiment.
55	1000		Dress and shields same as Udhlambedhlu (some have a bunch of split ostrich feathers back of head).	The Ngwekwe and Mhlenivu were at Nyezane, January 22, 1879.
55	500		Dress and shields same as Udhlambedhlu.	
64		4000	Dress same as the Usixepi, shields, white	Nodwengu is properly the name of the military kraal, but has come to be used for the corps. The Nodwengu corps were at Sandhlwana, January 22, 1879, and formed the extreme right of the Zulu centre.
54	500		Dress and shields same as Mkulutyane	
35	1500		Band of otter skin round forehead ; two plumes of the feathers of the Kafir finch on head, pointing backwards; ear-flaps of green monkey skin ; bunches of white cow-tails hanging from neck, down back and chest ; shields, black, with white spots.	
35	500		Dress and shields same as Ududulu	
54	1500		Band of otter-skin round forehead ; two white strips of dry cow-hide surmounted by the white tail of a cow on the head ; ear-flaps of green monkey-skin ; bunches of white cow-tails hanging from neck, down chest and back : shields, white.	
60	400	1000	Dress the same as the Udhlambedhlu, shields, white, with black and red spots	I have not included in the estimate of numbers, any men over the age of sixty. Thus, the first of the old regiments whose numbers will be given, is the Ndabakaomi.
55	600		Dress and shields the same as the Undabakaombi	

Corps, or Regiment having a Military Kraal.	Regiments composing Corps.	English Meaning of Name.	Who Raised by.	Name of Commanding Officer.	Name and Position of Military Kraal forming Head Quarters of Corps or Regiment.
Undi		Drakensberg	Cetywayo	Mnyamane	Ondine, about six miles ease of the ford over the West Umfolosi main road
	* Tulwana	Name of a Basuto chief, Usikwate's father	Umpande		Ondine
	* Nkonkone	Blue gnu	Umpande	Manzini	Ondine
	* Ndhlondhlo	Euphorbia	Umpande		Ondine
	Indluyengwe	Leopards' den	Umpande		Ondine
	Nkobamakosi	The bender of kings	Cetywayo	Usicweleewele	Old Ondine on the right bank of the Umhlatusi about seven miles S. of main road
*Udhloko		Name of a snake	Umpande	Usibepu	Qikazi—North of and close to Ondine
	Amakwenkwe		Umpande		Qikazi
Umbonambi or Nkonyanebomvu		The "Evil-seers" or "Red Calf"	Umpande	Nduvana	Umbonambi — on the coast, about fifteen miles S. of the entrance to St. Lucia Bay
	Amashutu	The "Loiterers"	Umpande		Umbonambi

Age of Men.	Number of Men in Regiment.	Number of Men in Corps.	*Distinguishing Regimental Marks.*	*Remarks.*
			None	The Undi is not the name of an original Regiment, after which the military kraal has been named, as is generally the case, but the designation given by Cetywayo to the Corps which includes the Royal Regiment—the Tulwana—as well as four others. The Undi corps were at Sandhlwana, January 22, 1879. The Tulwana, Ndhlonhlo, Nkonkone, and Indhluyengwe formed the Zulu right, and were but little in action. On the same day these regiments crossed the Buffalo River, the larger portion attacking Rorke's Drift post, where they were utterly defeated; the Indhluyengwe loosing about 1,000 men.
45	1500		Band of otter skin round forehead; two large plumes of the Kafir finch (Sakabuli) on either side of head; bunch of split ostrich feathers back of head (great men wear a bunch of the laurie's feathers); one long feather of the brown crane (Indwe) in centre of head; earflaps of green monkey-skin; large bunches of white cow-tails hanging from neck down chest and back; short kilt of civet-cat and green monkey skins fastened round waist, and reaching half-way to the knees, put on over ordinary dress; shields, white.	
43	500		Dress and shields same as Tulwana	
43	900	9900	Band of otter-skin round forehead; one long plume of the Kafir finch (Sakabuli) on forehead; small bunch of split feathers at back of head; ear-flaps of green monkey-skin; bunches of white cow tails suspended round neck, hanging down back and chest; short kilt, same as Tulwana; shield, same as Tulwana.	
28	1000		Band of leopard-skin round forehead (some have otter skin); large bunch of black split ostrich feathers front of head, surmounted by long white ostrich feathers[; two plumes of the Kafir finch (Sakabuli) on either side of head, pointing backwards; earflaps of green monkey-skin, and bunches of white cow-tails hanging from neck, over chest and back; shield, black, with white spot below.	
24	6000		Band of leopard-skin round forehead; two white cow-tails (they are sometimes black or red) raised on dry strips of white cow-hide on either side of head, fastened on by a strip of white cow-hide across forehead; two plumes of the Kafir finch (Sakabuli) on either side of head, pointing backwards; earflaps of green monkey-skin, and bunches of white cow-tails hanging from neck, down back and chest; shields, black, red, and spotted.	The Nkobamakosi regiment belongs to the Undi corps, but does not use the same military kraal as the rest. It formed the right of the Zulu left wing at Sandhlwana, where they are estimated to have lost 600.
10	2500	4000	Band of otter skin round forehead; one long feather of the blue crane (indwe) in front of head; ear flaps of green monkey skin, and bunches of white cow tails hanging from neck down back and chest; shields, red with white spot (some have white shields).	The Udhloko were with the Undi at Sandhlwana and Rorke's Drift, Jan. 22, 1879; their loss at these actions is estimated at 1,000 men.
29	1500			
32	1500	2000	Band of leopard skin across forehead; one plume of the Kafir finch in centre of head; ear flaps of green monkey skin, and bunches of white cow tails hanging from neck over back and chest; shields, black, and black with white spots.	The Umbonambi were at Sandhlwana, January 22, 1879, and formed the extreme left; their loss is estimated at 600 men.
32	500		Dress and shields same as the Umbonambi.	

Corps, or Regiment having a Military Kraal.	Regiments composing Corps.	English Meaning of Name.	Who Raised by.	Name of Commanding Officer.	Name and Position of Military Kraal forming Head Quarters of Corps or Regiment.
Umcityu		The "Sharp-pointed"	Umpande	Somcuba	Umkandampemvu—on the left bank of the W. Umfolosi, about four miles N.N.W. of Ondine
	Unqakamatye	"Stone-catchers"	Umpande		Ukandampemvu
	Umtulisazwi	"The peace-makers of the land"	Umpande	Uvumandaba	Ukandampemvu
Uve		Name of a bird	Cetywayo		Usindandhlovu—in the bush country about twelve miles S.S.E. of Ondine. Lately called Maiezekanye.
	*Umzinyati	Buffalo River	Umpande		Usindandhlovu

Total number of Zulu Army   ...   ...

NOTE.—All the regiments marked * are married men, wearing the head ring.

Age of Men.	Number of Men in Regiment.	Number of Men in Corps.	Distinguishing Regimental Marks.	Remarks.
28	2500	9000	Two long strips of white cow-hide with white cow-tails attached to their points on either side of head, secured by a roll of leopard skin across forehead; ear flaps of green monkey skin; two plumes of the Kafir finch (sakabuli) on either side of head, pointing back; bunches of white cow tails hanging from neck down chest and back; shields, black.	This corps is known as the Umcityu or Ukandapemvu (Redhead) indifferently. The name Umcityu is taken from a stick sharpened at both ends, because during the quarrel between Cetywayo and his brother Umbulaswi some of them took one side and some the other. The Umcityu were at Sandhlwana, January 22, 1879, and formed the left centre; their loss there is estimated at 800 men.
30	5000		Dress and shields same as Umcityu.	
29	1500		Dress and shields same as Umcityu.	
23	3500	4000	Dress and shields the same as the Nkobamakosi.	Usindandhlovu is the name of the military kraal lately built by Cetywayo, where the Umzinyati and Uve Regts. have been sent, without, however, having received any name but their regimental one. The Uve were at Sandhlwana, Jan. 22, 1879.
43	500		Band of the otter skin round forehead; long blue crane (indwa) feathers stuck in hair; ear flaps of green monkey skin; shields, white with black spots.	
				Note.—I have not put down the boy regiment now forming, as they are not yet regularly enrolled and have no military kraal, although tribally many of them have been fighting against us.
		41900		

ZULU HEADMEN.

Name of Chief.	Father.	Approx. Age.	Regiment.	Tribe.
Ohamu	Umpande	45	Tulwana	uZulu
Usiwetu	Umpande	45	Tulwana	uZulu
Usiteku	Umpande	43	Nkonkone	uZulu
Dabulamanzi	Umpande	35	Tulwana	uZulu
Ushingana	Umpande	40	Udhloko	uZulu
Umsuto	Umpande	35	Udududu	uZulu
Makwendu	Umpande	32	Umbonambi	uZulu
Umkihlana	Umpande	32	Umbonambi	uZulu
Umdabuko	Umpande	32	Ishutu	uZulu
Mahanana	Umpande	32	Ishutu.	uZulu
Usukane	Umpande	30	Nokenke	uZulu

Residence.	Remarks.
Mfemfe—about five miles north-west of the Ngomi Mountains.	Principal brother of the Zulu King. Has about 6,000 men, and is very rich in cattle. His district lies between the Ngomi Mountains and the Pongolo River, and is bounded by that of Mnyamana on the south and west, by Swaziland on the north, and on the east by Masipula. He advocates a different policy to Cetywayo, being the leader of the peace party, and is favourable to the English, though not to the Dutch. He is the most popular of the Princes, being liberal, good tempered, brave, and plain-spoken. A very large body of the Zulus would follow his lead in any disturbance, and he would possess considerable influence with the Natal Zulus. The European who would have the most influence with him would be Mr. Herbert Nunn, who for some years held a position with him similar to that held by Mr. John Dunn with Cetywayo.
Emkondo and Amateni—both on the east bank of the Black Umfolosi, near the Mbelebeleni kraal.	Next of importance to Ohamu. Was at one time Chief in command of Cetywayo's forces, before Umpande's death. Has not more than 500 men, and is poor for his rank. His district lies south of the Mbelebeleni kraal. Cetywayo's favourite brother, and the principal of the Princes who supported him in his struggle with Umbulaswi. Not favourably disposed to Europeans, and unpopular among the Zulus. He is a man of some ability, but mean and bad tempered.
Near Mr. Robinson's Mission Station, Magwaza.	Has about 400 men. His district lies on the Umhlatusi River, south-west of Magwaza. Of the same house as Ohamu, and next to him in rank in it. They have, however, quarrelled, and he now belongs to Cetywayo's party. He is popular, and possesses no inconsiderable influence.
On the east side of the Ntumeni Bush.	Has about 100 men. He belongs to Cetywayo's party. Is a great hunter, and a magnificent shot. A clever, unscrupulous, cruel, bad-tempered man, hated and feared by the Zulus. Was present at the actions at Sandhlwana, Rorke's Drift, and Ginginhlovu.
About five miles north of the Isixepi kraal.	Has very few people. A quiet inoffensive man. Belongs to Cetywayo's side of the house.
On the southern spurs of the Isihlalo hills.	Has about 150 men. Belongs to Cetywayo's side of the house
On the southern spurs of the Isihlalo hills.	Has very few men. Of the same house as Ohamu, and on good terms with him. Would probably support him in any disturbance. Is popular among the Zulus.
On the Isihlalo hills.	Has very few men. Belongs to Cetywayo's side of the house.
On the west bank of the Black Umfolosi, to the east of the Isihlalo hills.	Has very few men. Belongs to Cetywayo's side of the house
About five miles north of the Usixepi.	Has very few men. Belongs to Cetywayo's side of the house.
Near the junction of the Vuna River and the Black Umfolosi.	Has no men. An officer of the Nokenke Regiment. Belongs to Cetywayo's side of the house. Is so fat he can scarcely walk.

Name of Chief.	Father.	Approx. Age.	Regiment.	Tribe.
Usibepu	Mapita	35	Umxapo	(Amandblakazi) uZulu
Uhayana	Mapita	45	Tulwana	Ditto
Umhulungwana	Mapita	45	Tulwana	Ditto
Unobiya	Sotobe	75	Umlambongwenga	uZulu
Usiwangu	Umbikwana	78	Mbebebele	(Abaqulusi) uZulu
Mnyamano	Nqengelelo	60	Umkulutyana	Utelesi

Residence.	Remarks.
Northern portion of Mapita's country.	A cousin of the King. Is the commanding officer of the Udbloko Regiment. Has about 6,000 men. He is the principal son of the late great Chief Mapita, who had upwards of a hundred children, and he is the head of the Amandhlakazi tribe, Cetywayo's principal supporters in his struggle with Umbulaswi. He has of late years had several quarrels with the King, though none of great importance, and it is doubtful if he could be depended upon to support him. He is a man of intelligence and very quiet, having been among the most active in arming the Zulus, with whom he is now very popular. He bears a high character for civility to Europeans, and may be looked upon as favourably disposed to them.
Southern portion of Mapita's country.	A cousin of the King. Has about 4,000 men. The district belonging to Usibepu and Uhayana lies north of Somkeli, extending from the lower end of the uBombo to near the Black Umfolosi. Their people include a large number of Amatonga. He is the second great son of Mapita, holding a somewhat similar position to Usibepu to that held by Ohamu to Cetywayo, not being on particularly good terms with him, but being strong enough to hold his own. He is unpopular with everybody but the King, and although owning a large number of men, in case of a disturbance but few would follow him in opposition to his brother.
Mapita's country.	A cousin of the King. Has very few men. Dead.
Mavumingwana's district.	Is related to the King, but is favourable to Ohamu. A petty Chief under Mavumingwana, and an officer of the Umlambongwenya. His son married a sister of the King's, and he is very rich.
On the Bivana River, near the Dumbi Mountains.	Is appointed Chief of a portion of the Abaqulusi tribe, numbering about 500 men. Dead.
His principal kraal is on the Isikwebesi.	The Prime Minister of Zululand. His tribe musters about 11,000 men, but it does not bear any reputation for courage. His district is bounded by Ohamu and Masipula to the north, the Isebi tribe to the south, and by Tyingwayo and Mabamba on the west. He is extremely rich in cattle. Originally he was Cetywayo's greatest favourite, but of late years he has had several quarrels with him, and his influence, which had hitherto been very great, began perceptibly to decline towards the end of 1877. He is now said to be in alliance with Ohamu. The usual statement made by traders and missionaries in Zululand is that Mnyamane is a "stubborn Zulu," unfavourable to Europeans. There is, however, a cause for this. Mnyamane, as the great officer of State, and the representative of the King, does not consider it politic to give way to such Europeans as enter Zululand, unless in such demands as might receive the support of the English Government; but his determined action against the King, in conjunction with Ohamu and Umfusi, when Cetywayo wished to invade Swaziland soon after Sir Theophilus Shepstone's Coronation visit, not only proves his independence and power, but that, like Ohamu, he is unfavourable to the Zulu nation coming into collision with the British, unless when the former had manifestly right on their side. Under these circumstances, should war take place between Her Majesty's Government and Cetywayo, and should Ohamu come over to the English side, it is not at all improbable Mnyamane might join him. Though no doubt of an over-bearing and warlike disposition, he is a man eminently capable of following argument and listening to reason, nor likely to act without duly weighing circumstances and consequences. Was second in command at Kambula Hill, March 29, 1879.

Name of Chief.	Father.	Approx. Age.	Regiment.	Tribe.
Umfusi	Manyala	75	Umlambongwenya	Umhletye
Seketwayo	Unhlaka	65	Nodwengu	Umhlalosi
Untuzwa	Unhlaka	70	Undabakaombi	Umhlalosi
Tyingwayo	Maholo	68	Udhlambedhlu	Koza
Mqokwane	Manyosi	70	Isixepi	Mambateni
Umzi	Manyosi	40	Tulwana	Mambata
Umfinyeli	Nguzalele	80	Isanda	Xulo
Unkabanina	Umbopa	45	Tulwana	Hlabisa
Abantubensumo	Zwane	45	Tulwana	Utelezi
Umkosana	Umvundhlana	43	Ndhlondhlo	Biyela
Umgitywa	Umvundhlana	45	Tulwana	Biyela
Faku	Ziningo	45	Tulwana	Ntombela
Umatyana	Usityakuza		Undabakaombi	Amacunu
Usipeku	Umxamana	55	Isanqu	Kumalo
Umatyiya	Umtyandu	60	Undabakaombi	Unzuzu

Residence.	Remarks.
Mapeta's district.	The commanding officer of the Umlambongwenya Regiment. Has very few people. A tall, spare man, with a great reputation for courage, and a teetotaller. He would follow the lead of Usibepu.
Above Usirayo, on the Blood River.	The commanding officer of the Nodwengu Regt. Has about 3,000 men. Is, from the position of his district, very bitter against the Dutch, and would probably join the war party.
Seketwayo's district.	The commanding officer of the Umbonambi Regt. Has about 300 men. A brother of Seketwayo, and said to be very warlike.
Near the Ntabankulu mountain.	Second Minister in Zululand. Has about 1,500 men. Second in command of the Qikazi military kraal. Is a great friend of Mnyamane's, and would probably follow his lead. He has, however, until lately always been held in more or less suspicion by the King, as being the officer who was sent down by Umpande with the Isanqu Regiment at the time of the battle of the Tugela, to, it was said, assist Umbulaswi. He is a warlike man, and is said to be very cruel. Was second in in command at Sandhlwana, and commanded the attack at Kambula Hill, March 29, 1879.
The country round the Isihlalo hills.	Commanding officer of the Usixepi Regiment. Has very few men.
The country round the Isihlalo hills.	Head of Manyosi's tribe. Numbering about 500 men. Killed at Sandhlwana.
On the Mona River, in Mapeta's district.	A body servant of Umpande's, and so very old that he took leave of the King at the last feast of first fruits.
Near Emangweni and mouth of the Umhlatusi River.	Has a small tribe. Said to be the strongest man in Zululand. A friend and political follower of Usirayo. A turbulent, restless man, who came into power but recently, and is disliked by the principal officers and chief men of the nation.
On the Pongolo, close to Ohamu's district.	A petty chief under Mnyamane.
Below the Malabatini, west of Somkeli.	Has about 3,000 men. Would remain loyal to Cetywayo, but is strongly opposed to the war policy of Usirayo. He was killed at Sandhlwana leading the Umcityu Regiment. His principal son is Umnqeto, who succeeds. Killed in the action on 22nd January.
Near the Ngoye mountains, in Umkosana's district.	A younger brother of Umkosana, and has about 1,000 men under his direct authority.
East of Isipezi hill.	Has very few people. His head kraal is on the wagon road.
Below Usirayo, on the Natal border.	An officer of the Undabakaombi Regiment. Has about 800 men. His principal kraal, Dayingubo, is on the wagon road from Rorke's Drift, at the Umhlatusi River. Is favourable to the English; being very rich and the King having illtreated him. His son, Umizo, married a sister of the King.
Near the Entumeni.	An officer of the Isanqu. A quarrelsome violent man. He is a great friend of Prince Udabulamanzi, but has no influence with the people generally.
Nyezane.	An officer of the Undabakaombi Regiment. Has about 600 men. His head kraal, Emfeni, is close to the wagon road on the right, at the first cutting going up to the Etshowe after leaving the flat. Is a connection by marriage of the present King, and buried the late one. Has a very quarrelsome tribe. Was in command of the portion of the Zulu force at Nyezane on January 22, 1879.

Name of Chief.	Father.	Approx. Age.	Regiment.	Tribe.
Ugebula		70	Nodwengu	Neni
Usambela	Umzimba	45	Tulwana	Unzuza
Umfanawendhlela	Manzine	70	Udhloko	Uzungu
Umavumingwana	Umzimba	45	Tulwana	
Umqandi	Matyana	45	Tulwana	Utelezi
Ufokoti	Sokufonce		Nkonkone	Xulo
Uluhungu	Sotobi	70	Isixepi	Amacubo
Ubandamana	Ndhlela	45	Tulwana	Untuli
Udwaba	Mpunzi		Undabakaombi	uZungu
Umvemve			Nhlondhlo	
Sombityana	Uyoto		Nhlondhlo	Xabashi
Matyana	Mondisa		Undabakaombi	Amacunu
Manqondo	Zwane	90		Makwaza
Mageza	Umthsito	64	Nodwengu	Amagungebi
Umtyegula	Nogwaza	45	Tulwana	Usibiya
Umsiyane	Umhlana	90		Xulo
Umpezeni	Nganqa		Nodwengu	Biyela
Usigidi	Matanda			
Umadwaba	Ndhlaludaka		Nodwengu	Nzuza

Residence.	Remarks.
North-west of Makwaza Mission Station.	Has very few people. An officer of the Qikazi military kraal. One of the political messengers of the late King, but not a favourite of Cetywayo's. Was one of the Zulu representatives at the meeting at the Lower Tugela ford, December 11th, 1878.
East side of the Matikulu River.	His chief kraal is on the east side of the Matikulu River, three miles from the wagon drift on the left hand side of the road. Has very few people. Is a body-servant of the King's.
Southern spurs of the Isihlalo.	Has about 200 men. From his head kraal, Ntandakuwela, a footpath goes down to the Sindandhlovu kraal, about seven miles, passing through a very broken country covered with thorn bush. Is second in command of the Udhloko regiment.
In Umkosana's district.	
East side of Ndhlazatye at source of Itaka River.	An officer of the Isebi kraal. *Present at the delivery of the ultimatum. 11.11.79.*
In Matyana ka Mondisa's country.	Is a body-servant of the King's.
West side of the Nkandhla, on the Nsuzi River, in Sokufa's district.	Second in command of the Isixepi Regiment. Has a few men under Sokufa.
Mavumingwana's district.	An officer of the Tulwane. Petty chief under Mavumingwana.
Southern corner of Usirayo's district.	Petty chief under Usirayo.
Southern part of Usirayo's district.	Petty chief under Usirayo.
Under the Isipezi, about one mile from the wagon road.	Petty chief under Usirayo. A body-servant of the King's.
Below Matyana ka Usityakuza, and all round the Iqudeni, where his principal kraal is.	Has about 700 men. Is a refugee and outlaw from Natal, and has married two sisters of the King's.
Has a strip of country lying between the junction of the Buffalo and Tugela Rivers and the Nsuze. His principal kraal is in the Tugela Valley, about the junction of the Nsuzi.	Is too old for any service. Has about 1,500 men. His people are very hostile to the whites. He had two sons killed at Kambula Hill on March 29th, 1879.
North-east of the Matonkulum'n, on the sources of the Black Umfolozi.	A petty chief. A favourite of the late King; would follow Ohamu.
On the Umkuzi, at the point where Ohamu and Masipula's Counties join.	Ohamu's principal chief. Has about 500 men.
Ohamu's district on the Ngomi mountains.	A very old chief, having sons seventy years of age. Has about 800 men. His principal son is very loyal to Ohamu.
Close to the right of the wagon road, south of Etchowe.	Petty chief under King.
Near the junction of the Nzuze and Tugela Rivers.	Petty chief under Mavumingwana.
On the Matikulu, two miles left of drift.	Petty chief under King.

Name of Chief.	Father.	Approx. Age.	Regiment.	Tribe.
Upakade	Amandhlasilo		Undabakaombi	Elangeni
Ubilibana	Bangela		Bulawayo	Makwaza
Upalane	Umdinwa		Umkulutyana	Puqanyoni
Umkanyile	Fusa			uZulu
Umgebisa	Ntyoko	70	Usixepi	Makoba
Umaziyana	Boja	45	Tulwana	Umpungosi
Umatondwana	Nogwaza	90	Kufasimba	Gazu
Usirayo	Xongo	55	Undabakaombi	Amaquneli
Umankayana	Ndhlaka	60	Undabakaombi	Umhlalosi
Pakade	Ungonela	28	Indhluyengwe	Umpungosi
Uqetuka	Manqondo	60	Undabakaombi	Makwaza
Umabusi	Situnga	60	Udududu	Biyela
Somkeli	Malanda	40	Nkonkone	Mpuganyoni
Umlandela	Umbiya	70	Impohlo	Umtetwa
Usigodi	Masipula	28	Umcityu	Umgazi
Gausi	Silwana	60	Undabakaombi	Umpungozi

Residence.	Remarks.
Two miles west of Magwaza.	An officer of the Nkobamakosi Regiment. A man much disliked, having murdered his father.
Between the Nsuzi and the Nkandhla.	A petty chief under Manqondo.
Between the Mpangeni River and Emangweni kraal, near the wagon road.	Is officer in charge of the Hlangezwa tribe, belonging to the King, numbering about 1,000 men. *Present at delivery of ultimatum 11. 11. 78.*
Near the Umpangisweni kraal, in Mnyamane's country.	Dead—left a son.
On west side of the Ndulindi.	A petty chief with very few people. Has been in Natal as a refugee, but returned to Zululand in 1871.
On the west side of the Umhlatusi valley, on right hand side of the wagon road.	A petty chief under Gausi. A favourite of the King's.
Maqondo's district.	A petty chief under Manqondo.
On Buffalo border, chief kraal, "Usokexe," opposite Rorke's Drift. Said to be fortified.	Is the chief of the King's household, and an officer of the Undabakaombi Regiment. Has about 3,000 men. The King's greatest favourite. It was by his advice that the King purchased guns, and horses were first introduced by him into Zululand. His tribe is said to be very warlike. He is said to be of a treacherous and cunning character, and is disliked by the other chiefs.
Gausi's district.	
Gausi's district. His chief kraal is three miles south of the separation of the Makwaza and Undi roads coming from Rorke's Drift, and a quarter of a mile off the road.	A petty chief under Gausi. Is an officer of the Ndhluyengwe Regiment.
In Sokufa's district, between Nkandhla mountains and Umhlatusi River.	Chief son of Manqondo, and is second in command of the Undi Corps. Has no people. Is unfavourable to whites.
In Mavumingwana's country, near the sources of the Imvuzani Rivers.	A petty chief. An officer of the Udududu.
South of Mapita's country.	An officer of the Tulwane. Has about 8,000 men. A first cousin of the King's, and on good terms with him. He is very favourable to whites, and is an easy-going quiet man, averse to war.
Between Somkeli and Umkosana.	Has about 2,000 men. He married a sister of the late King, and his son, Usokwatyata, belonging to the Umxapo Regt. is a cousin of Cetywayo, with whom he is on good terms.
On the south bank of the Umkusi River, in Masipula's country.	Has about 4,000 men. Killed at Sandhlwana. Chief son of the Masipula. Prime Minister of Zululand under Umpande. Is favourable to Ohamu. Died at his home of a wound received in the attack at Sandhlwana on January 22, 1879.
Principal kraal close to left of wagon road, three miles beyond the Umlalasi River.	An officer of the Undi. Has about 5,000 men. His district lies south of the Amahlabati, being bounded by Umkosana to the east, and by Umhlongolwana to the south. A great favourite of the King, though a leader of the peace party. Is a cripple from paralysis.

Name of Chief.	Father.	Approx. Age.	Regiment.	Tribe.
Umhlongolwana	Sababa	80	Umgundhlovu	Biyela
Sokufa	Sotobi	95	Umlanbongwanya	Amacubi
Usikananda	Sokufa	60	Umkulutyane	Amacubi
Untubeni	Umsholoza	80	Ihlaba	Amacubi
Hlomuza	Mapita	45	Tulwana	Amandhlakazi (uZulu)
Melelesi	Manyosi	60	Umkulutyane	Mambata
Mabamba	Lukwazi	32	Umbonambi	Ntombela
Magumdane	Xongo	68	Udhlambedhlu	Amaqunebi
Unguqa	Umpundulwana	60	Undabakaombi	Telezi
Umvumandaba	Unteti	60	Umkulutyane	Biyela
Umavumingwana	Ndhlela	40	Tulwana	Untuli
Ubizo	Umzimba	45	Tulwana	Umhletye
Ugodide	Ndhlela	70	Nyosi	Untuli
Mabilwane	Mahlanganisa	75	Umlambongwenya	Amaqungebi
Masegwane	Sopigwasi	55	Isanqu	Mambateni
Ugangasa	Macingwane	53	Umhlenivu	nZulu
Umsuto	Silwane	60	Undabakaombi	Umpungosi
Habana	Umzwageli	55	Isanqu	Dubi
Manyonyo	Zongolo	60	Undabakaombi	Umhletye
Usieweleewele	Umhlegehlege	53	Umhlenivu	Mangata

Residence.	Remarks.
His principal kraal is close to Magwaza, Mr. Robertson's Mission Station.	Has about 1,000 men. Is second in command of the Bulawayo. His district lies south of Gausi and east of the Umhlatusi. Would probably follow Umkosana. The Rev. R. Robertson would have influence with him.
Principal kraal south of the wagon road to the Empandhlani on the west bank of the Umhlatusi.	Is a very old man. Has about 1,000 men. The Amacubi tribe has never been conquered by the Zulus.
Sokufa's district.	Chief son of Sokufa. Has been a refugee in Natal and a policeman. He returned to Zululand eight years ago Favourable to whites.
Nkandhla.	Petty chief under Sokufa. Has about 150 men.
Mapita's district.	The third son of Mapita in point of influence.
Near Isihlalo hill.	Second in command of the Nodwengu.
South of the Bivane stream, where it joins the Pongolo.	Has a tribe of about 3,000 men, who have, under him, been actively fighting the column of Col. Wood, V.-C., C.B.
Under the Malakata hill in Usirayo's district.	Is the principal son of Xongo, and has only become of secondary importance to his brother Usirayo on account of his weakness of character. Gave himself up to No. 3 column, with about thirty men, shortly before the battle of Sandhlwana.
Left bank Black Umfolosi River, twenty miles from Undi.	An officer of the Umcityu Regiment.
On left bank of the Mfule.	Second in command of the Umcityu Regiment. *Present it delivery of ultimatum 11.11.78*
Mpapala.	Commands the Undi corps, and was commander-in-chief of the Zulu army which attacked No. 3 column, Jan. 22, 1879.
On the right of the Amangwe kraal on the left of the Umhlatusi.	An officer of the Nokenke, and a small chief, having about 400 men.
Between the Nsuzi River and the Tugela.	Commanding officer of the Uhlambedhlu Regiment. Has a large tribe, about 1,000 men. Has been a refugee in Natal. Is a brother of Mavumingwana.
On the left bank of the Matikulu, near J. Dunn's wagon road.	Commanding officer of the Umginginhlovu military kraal. Is a petty chief with but few men. Was in command of the Umginginhlovu Contingent at the action with No. 1 column at the Nyezane on January 22, 1879, and at Ginginhlovu, April 2, 1879. *Present at delivery of ultimatum 11.11.78*
On the left bank of the Matikulu, close to its mouth.	A body-servant of the King's. Was in command of a portion of the force at the action at the Nyezane on January 22, 1879, and was present at Ginginhlovu, April 2, 1879.
Near the upper part of the Isikwebesi River.	Is second in command of the Uve Regiment.
On the Umkukusi stream, on right of wagon road to Etshowe.	Is an officer of the Uve.
On right bank of the Umhlatusi to south of main wagon road.	Is chief of the Dubi tribe, and an Officer of the Nkobamakosi. Has about 500 men. Lived originally in Natal.
Between the Umhlatusi and the Umhlatuzana River.	Has about 200 men. Is an officer of the Nkobamakosi.
On the left bank of the Umhlatusi River, opposite Makwaza.	Commanding officer of the Nkobamakosi Regiment. Belongs to the war party.

Name.	Father.	Approx. Age.	Regiment.	Tribe.
Unohadu	Umswele	80	Mtontela	Xulo
Umcelu	Silwane	60	Undabakaombi	Umpungosi
Upuxe	Tyoko		Mhlenivu	Makoba
Mundula	Somapunga		Nodwengu	Ndwandwe
Umgebisa ·	Tyoko		Impothlo	Makoba
Somopo	Zikala			Matembi
Mahubulwana	Udumizela		Ndhlokonkulu	Abaqulusi
Umtakati	Udukuzana		Ukandampemvu	Abaqulusi
Umsebe	Madaka		Tulwana	Abaqulusi
Umcwayo	Mangeda		Not enrolled	Abaqulusi
Usikobobo	Mababakezana		Nsukamgeni	Abaqulusi
Unani	Utangazela		Umkwenkwe	Abaqulusi
Usityaluza	Mamba		Udhlambedhla	Umgazi
Majumba	Masipula		Ngobamakosi	Umgazi
Uyeyeza	Umkatyu		Inkulutyana	Amandhlakazi
Nsuza			Impohlo	Amandhlakazi
Maputwana			Impohlo	Amandhlakazi

Residence.	Remarks.
On the right bank of the Umhlatusi River, opposite to Gausi's district.	Has a tribe of about 300 men. Dead. Is succeeded by Mapungwana of the Tulwana Regiment.
Right bank of Umlalasi stream, south of wagon road.	A brother of Gausi. Was a body-servant of the King's. Was wounded at Nyezane January 22, 1879, and afterwards died.
Right bank of Matikulu.	A junior officer of the Umhlinivu. Was killed at Nyezane on January 22, 1879.
On the left bank of the Umkusi River valley before it reaches the duBombo valley.	Commanding officer of the Nodwengu corps. Has about 700 men. *Present at delivery of ultimatum 11. 12. 78.*
Right bank of Matikulu.	Second in command of the Usixepi kraal, and a relation by marriage of the King's. Crossed into Natal at the time of the battle of the Tugela, and re-crossed in 1873. Many of his people remained in Natal. Has only about 100 men.
	Commanding officer of the Amangwe military kraal. Was in command at attack at Ginginhlovu, April 2, 1879.
Amahlabatini district.	This district was originally occupied by the Abaqulusi. This man and Umtakati are the two principal officers of the Abaqulusi. *Present at delivery of ultimatum.*
Under the Ityongololo hill.	Near the Abaqulusini military kraal, lately destroyed by Col. Buller.
Under Hlobana mountain.	He is a second cousin of Cetywayo's, being a great grandson of Jama.
Eastern side of Ityenteka Neck.	He is a grandson of a Chief conquered by Tyaka named Uhawana, after whom the mountain, Nqaba-ka-Hawana, is named.
On the Bivana River, near the Idumbi mountain.	
Ditto.	
On the Umkusi River, below Ohamu's.	He is a brother of Masipula, and was guardian to Usigodi (heir to Masipula), who died at his home of a wound received at Isandhlwana, January 22, 1879.
Ditto.	Next in succession to Usigodi. Was wounded in the foot at Isandhlwana.
In the Pongolo River valley, near the Bomba mountains.	
Ditto.	
Ditto.	

Name of Chief.	Father.	Approx. Age.	Regiment.	Tribe.
Usintwangu Umbopa	Usitayi		Umoduvangu	Hlabisa
Umpepa				
Somcityu				
Mohila				
Mongena ~~Umahabulwana~~				
Umgulugulu ~~Umapa~~				
Umzwakali				
Umkiyane	Sambane			
Umhlekwane	Myati			
Utafiyiya	Matangata			

Residence	Remarks
	was present at the delivery of the ultimatum
South of lower road across the Matikulu. Left bank.	Principal messenger of Cetywayo. 19.11.78
East bank Black Umfolozi close above junction of the Umona stream.	Uncle of Umpande's mother. Was an officer of Umpande's household.
	C.O. of Uve regt. Present at delivery of ultimatum. 19.11.78. Killed at Ginginhlovo 2.4.79.
	Present at delivery of ultimatum 11.11.78
	Present at delivery of ultimatum 11.11.78
	Present at delivery of ultimatum 11.11.78.
	Present at delivery of ultimatum 11.11.78
	Present at delivery of ultimatum 11.11.78
Valley between Ngwe and the Matankulu.	
	C.O. of Isangu regt. Killed at Kambula
	Second in command of right wing of Tulwane regt. Killed at Kambula.

25047179R00024

Printed in Great Britain
by Amazon